HOW TO TELL IF YOUR
BOYFRIEND IS
THE ANTICHRIST

To the lovely Kimmy,

I figured this guide would come in handy, seeing as you and I can clearly not tell whether we are, in fact, dating any of the following: Pathologic liars, crackheads, alcoholics, hit men, regaeholics, polygamists, ex-cons, cult leaders, trekkies, bastards, pimps or the antichris. Now we will be able to tell. You know... for next time.

Much love!

HOW TO TELL IF YOUR
BOYFRIEND IS
THE ANTICHRIST

(and if he is, should you
break up with him?)

BY PATRICIA CARLIN
ILLUSTRATED BY MICHAEL MILLER

QUIRK BOOKS

PHILADELPHIA

Library of Congress Cataloging in Publication Number: 2006932064

ISBN: 978-1-59474-140-1

Printed in China
Typeset in Goudy and ITC Legacy Sans

Designed by Karen Onorato
Illustrations by Michael Miller
Edited by Melissa Wagner
Production management by Stephanie O'Neill McKenna

Distributed in North America by Chronicle Books
85 Second Street
San Francisco, CA 94105

10 9 8 7 6 5 4 3 2 1

Quirk Books
215 Church Street
Philadelphia, PA 19106
www.quirkbooks.com

TABLE OF CONTENTS

Introduction 11

How to Tell If Your Boyfriend Is . . .

The Antichrist 12
Obsessive-Compulsive 14
A Closeted Homosexual 15
Suffering from Amnesia 17
A Pimp 18
Actually Twins 19
An Extraterrestrial 20
A Commitment-phobe 22
A Total Bastard 23
Suffering from ADHD 25
A Serial Killer 26
An Enabler 27
A Kleptomaniac 28
A Robot 30
A Scientologist 31
A Trekkie 33
A Hypochondriac 34
A Slacker 35
A Time Traveler from the Past 36
A Misanthrope 38
A Misogynist 39
Actually a Woman 41
In the Witness Protection Program 42

TABLE OF CONTENTS

Passive-Aggressive 43
A Cult Leader................................ 44
Suffering from an Anxiety Disorder 46
A Zombie.................................... 47
A Polygamist 49
An Ex-Convict................................ 50
Too Old for You.............................. 51
A Rageaholic 52
A Junkie 54
An Illegal Alien 55
Possessed by Demons 57
A Workaholic................................ 58
A Pedophile 59
A Bumpkin.................................. 60
Suffering from Multiple Personality Disorder..... 62
A Player 63
A Fugitive from Justice 65
Jealous..................................... 66
A Hit Man 67
Married with Children 68
A Ghost 70
An Alcoholic................................. 71
A Stalker.................................... 73
A Psychic 74
On Crystal Meth 75
A Cross-Dresser 76

TABLE OF CONTENTS

A Nymphomaniac 78
A Narcissist 79
Addicted to Porn 81
Bipolar 82
A Mama's Boy 83
An Angel 84
A Government-Trained Assassin 86
Dyslexic 87
A Renegade Cop 89
Clinically Depressed 90
Suffering from an STD 91
Narcoleptic 92
A Control Freak 94
P-Whipped 95
On Steroids 97
A Homophobe 98
A Compulsive Gambler 99
A Gun Nut 100
A Vampire 102
Trying to Kill You 103
Agoraphobic 105
An Insufferable Bore 106
A Crackhead 107
A Pathological Liar 108
Index by Trait 109
Acknowledgments 112

To all the men I've loved before.

INTRODUCTION

Let's face it. Lust can severely impair your judgment. So when you meet a hot new guy, it may be hard to tell the difference between a quirk and a severe personality disorder. Is he a pedophile or just great with children? Can you ever really know for sure? Probably not without a hidden camera.

But luckily, there are some early warning signs. And if you're looking for love, it's crucial that you learn to identify those signs immediately. That's where this essential guide comes in. Sort of a cross between *The Rules*, *He's Just Not That Into You*, and the *Diagnostic and Statistical Manual of Mental Disorders*, it teaches you to instantly spot all kinds of dangerous personality types, including serial killers, stalkers, pimps, and Scientologists.

More importantly, it offers valuable tips on how to quickly and safely dump them, so you can exit a bad relationship before it even starts. That's *before* you wind up with a drinking problem, a criminal record, or multiple stab wounds. Talk about empowerment.

The point is not to frighten you into permanent single status. It's simply this: If you want to find your soulmate, you have to make informed romantic choices. So don't get down on love. But don't let yourself get tossed into a shallow grave behind the interstate, either. You'll never meet a nice guy *there*.

HOW TO TELL IF YOUR BOYFRIEND IS
THE ANTICHRIST

✓ Never says "God bless you" when you sneeze.

✓ Unmoved by WWJD.

✓ Drives an SUV with a fish bumper sticker.

✓ Doesn't recycle.

✓ Is self-conscious about his cloven hooves.

Should you break up with him? So you did the Prince of Darkness. Does it make you a bad person? Not necessarily, but your morals are weak at best. Which is exactly what he's looking for in a woman.

But ultimately, it's not your body he wants, no matter how hot you are. He's actually after nothing less than your soul, and not to cherish and nurture, either—rather, to torture relentlessly in the everlasting fires of hell. So unless you're into that sort of thing, break up now.

If you do decide to stay and give him what he wants, consider yourself warned. As soon as he's finished with you, he'll move on to his next conquest without a backward glance. He'll leave you roasting on a spit for all eternity, kicking yourself for your own selfish, destructive choices. Right next to those girls from your junior-high gym class, the Hummer marketing people, and Karl Rove.

HOW TO TELL IF YOUR BOYFRIEND IS
OBSESSIVE-COMPULSIVE

✓ Your water bill has increased 400 percent since he moved in.

✓ Your face is chafed where he kissed you good-bye eighty-seven times.

✓ He has to clap ten times and touch his nose before he can have an orgasm.

Should you break up with him? Tough call. On the plus side, you can absolutely count on him. He certainly follows a set routine. And he doesn't have much time to cheat between the hand-washings. However, his extracurricular activities may leave little time for you. If you do choose to break up, be persistent—you may have to tell him more than once before it "takes."

HOW TO TELL IF YOUR BOYFRIEND IS
A CLOSETED HOMOSEXUAL

✓ Has a gym buddy.

✓ Keeps stealing the Abercrombie catalog.

✓ Watches Meg Ryan movies with you instead of the play-offs.

✓ Is content to cuddle most nights, because he had sex at a rest stop on the way home.

Should you break up with him? It's a shame, really. You like your "boyfriend" so much. You laugh. You shop. You stay up all night talking. You watch *The O.C.* together. You've just got so much in common—all but one little thing. Testicles. And that's a definite dealbreaker. So unless you sprout a pair after reading this, move on. You can still laugh and shop together. Just remember to make yourself available to the heterosexual male population for the committed relationship you so richly deserve. Or, at the very least, for wild, anonymous sex.

See also: Scientologist, p. 31

HOW TO TELL IF YOUR BOYFRIEND IS
SUFFERING FROM AMNESIA

✓ Surprisingly little baggage.

✓ Simple name (i.e., Bob Spoon, Jack Jackson).

✓ You found him wandering the streets with a bandage on his head.

✓ Honestly perplexed about the origin of his tattoo.

✓ Doesn't think he's ever loved like this before.

Should you break up with him? Are you kidding? He's a clean slate. You can dress him how you like, you choose all the movies, and he has no annoying friends or family. Jackpot! The only downsides are: (1) he could regain his memory, and with it, some control of the relationship; and (2) his family and/or friends may find and reclaim him. But they might not recognize him with the makeover you gave him. Keep him while you can.

See also: Time Traveler from the Past, p. 36; Suffering from Multiple Personality Disorder, p. 62

HOW TO TELL IF YOUR BOYFRIEND IS
A PIMP

✓ You met him at the bus station the day you arrived from Kansas.

✓ Thinks high school is for suckers, too.

✓ Asks you to stop at the drugstore to pick up some roofies on your way home.

Should you break up with him? If you're going to be a ho, be your own ho. If you don't want to be a ho, don't talk to men hanging around bus stations. When you're older—say, eighteen or nineteen—you'll understand that. Get away from this guy immediately. And this isn't a breakup, it's really more of an escape, so treat it as such. Run back to the nearest cornfield and stay there till you're thirty.

HOW TO TELL IF YOUR BOYFRIEND IS
ACTUALLY TWINS

✓ Changes his mind a lot.

✓ That freckle keeps moving.

✓ Sometimes he looks five minutes older.

Should you break up with him? These two will certainly keep you on your toes. They're into playing games. If you are too, try this one out: Tell your boyfriend that you've got some exciting news. You're expecting his baby! Of course you're planning to keep it. Does he want to get married or simply kick in for child support for the next twenty years? Then sit back and allow the finger pointing to begin. Ha. Games are fun.

See also: Suffering from Multiple Personality Disorder, p. 62

HOW TO TELL IF YOUR BOYFRIEND IS
AN EXTRATERRESTRIAL

✓ It's easy to get lost in his large, soulful eyes.

✓ You can't seem to remember what you do with him, although you spend large chunks of time together.

✓ Anally probed you on the first date.

Should you break up with him? You are the submissive in this relationship, so it's really not up to you. If it were, the answer would be yes, because this guy, or being, is a user. You fit some prototype of a typical human female, and he's simply gathering intelligence. When the mission is complete, you will be released, so in the meantime, try not to bring about the destruction of the species. And don't forget the birth control, unless you want a fetus exploding from your abdomen sometime soon.

HOW TO TELL IF YOUR BOYFRIEND IS
A COMMITMENT-PHOBE

✓ Longs for his carnie days.

✓ Introduces you as his "current" girlfriend.

✓ Loses his erection when that diamond commercial comes on.

✓ No tattoos or piercings of any kind.

✓ He's working as a temp, for now.

Should you break up with him? It may not be necessary. First, confirm that you are really in a "relationship." It could be that what you consider to be a committed, exclusive romance is what he considers to be friends with benefits. If you determine that it is in fact a relationship, go ahead and break up, because he's clearly keeping all his options open. Just stop calling. He won't care.

HOW TO TELL IF YOUR BOYFRIEND IS
A TOTAL BASTARD

✓ Asks you to watch his kids while he takes out his other girlfriend.

✓ Argues that it's not his fault he wrecked your car, because he was drunk.

✓ Thinks you do look fat in those jeans.

✓ Tells you to call him when you're not "on the rag."

✓ Strangled your puppy when you forgot to pick up his smokes.

Should you break up with him? Is he really just a hurt little boy at heart? Maybe. But he's a *mean* little boy. Don't be tempted to think you can change him. He'll only turn you into a mean bastard, too. Break up.

HOW TO TELL IF YOUR BOYFRIEND IS
SUFFERING FROM ADHD

✓ You've trained yourself to come in thirty seconds or less.

✓ Constantly reintroduces himself to your friends.

✓ 485 exes, approximately.

✓ Wishes he had time for a microwave burrito.

Should you break up with him? It's a whirlwind romance. This guy has a lot going on. It seems exciting till you realize he actually never accomplishes anything. It's like dating a hamster on a wheel. Frankly speaking, Ritalin is the only hope for this relationship. So crush a couple and sprinkle them in his Red Bull. If you don't see a change in a couple of weeks, break up. And don't feel bad if he replaces you right away. It's nothing personal.

HOW TO TELL IF YOUR BOYFRIEND IS
A SERIAL KILLER

✓ Your cat has some unexplained injuries.

✓ After your first night together, your breath smells of chloroform.

✓ Cuts up your *InStyle* to compose manifestos.

✓ You always have to take your car, because his has no passenger seat.

Should you break up with him? In a word, yes. This is one of the few cases where it's entirely appropriate to break up over the phone. Preferably from an undisclosed location, several hundred miles away.

See also: Hit Man, p. 67; Trying to Kill You, p. 103

HOW TO TELL IF YOUR BOYFRIEND IS
AN ENABLER

✓ Doesn't need to know where your furniture went—that's your business.

✓ Keeps the car running while you score.

✓ Agrees that your caseworker lacks a sense of humor.

Should you break up with him? He really, truly understands you, doesn't he? He's there for you no matter what, and he never comes down on you like those other bitches. So why would you want to break up? Unconditional support is very hard to come by in this cold, cold world. Isn't that why you're smoking/drinking/using/gambling in the first place?

HOW TO TELL IF YOUR BOYFRIEND IS
A KLEPTOMANIAC

✓ Tries to pass off the store sensor on his shirt as an oversized cufflink.

✓ Won't let you wear your birthday present to his sister's house.

✓ Has several monogrammed towels, but they're not the same monograms.

✓ Wishes he could keep on top of the clutter at his place.

Should you break up with him? The klepto is often misunderstood. Okay, he's a petty thief, but he's only doing it for the thrill. He steals flatware not because he needs it, but for the adrenaline rush. And he won't stop unless he can replace that behavior with something equally exciting. Snowboarding. Cliff-diving. Running yellow lights. Making crank calls. It really doesn't matter, as long as it doesn't impact your social life. Because your friends will be understanding, but there are limits. Nobody wants to feel compelled to frisk the guests after a dinner party. If you can't change him, move along.

HOW TO TELL IF YOUR BOYFRIEND IS
A ROBOT

✓ Never loses his temper.

✓ The sex is, well, a little mechanical.

✓ You can tell him anything, because he's so nonjudgmental.

✓ Cold hands and feet.

Should you break up with him? He's safe; he's predictable. That's not necessarily a bad thing. But what about passion? What about love? Well, marrying for love is a relatively recent phenomenon. And with a 50 percent divorce rate, it may be ill-advised. Stick it out. Perhaps the Stepford Men's Club was ahead of its time.

See also: Workaholic, p. 58

HOW TO TELL IF YOUR BOYFRIEND IS
A SCIENTOLOGIST

✓ He's a major motion picture star.

✓ For Valentine's Day, he gives you *Battlefield Earth*, director's cut.

✓ Claims to be your thetan-mate.

✓ Used to date Kirstie Alley.

✓ Killed a psychiatrist.

Should you break up with him? Break up before he forces you to bear his children in total silence. It's easy. Just tell him you're taking antidepressants.

See also: Cult Leader, p. 44; Extraterrestrial, p. 20

HOW TO TELL IF YOUR BOYFRIEND IS
A TREKKIE

✓ Spock ears in the underwear drawer.

✓ Lapses into Klingon during orgasm.

✓ Tried to kick your ass when you claimed to prefer
Voyager. But couldn't.

✓ You're his first.

Should you break up with him? *Star Trek* is a fairly harmless obsession. But if you don't share it, it could eventually come between the two of you. So start watching the stupid show with him. See if you can get into it. If it weirds you out, break up.

He might curse your Romulan ways, but just brush it off. He's hurt. And if you change your mind and want him back, pick up the phone and give him a call. Don't worry—he'll be available.

HOW TO TELL IF YOUR BOYFRIEND IS
A HYPOCHONDRIAC

✓ It says so on his med-alert bracelet.

✓ Razes all trees on his property to reduce the risk of contracting bird flu.

✓ Keeps the World Health Organization on his speed dial.

✓ Introduced you to dental dams.

✓ Bugs you to check his moles.

Should you break up with him? He won't let you wear low-cut tops because you might catch cold. He won't eat sushi because he might get worms. With him, the glass is always half empty and teeming with bacteria. Break up with him and celebrate by having unprotected sex with a stranger.

See also: Suffering from an Anxiety Disorder, p. 46

HOW TO TELL IF YOUR BOYFRIEND IS
A SLACKER

✓ Those aren't dimples, they're sheet wrinkles.

✓ Goes on for hours about the relative merits of
  Halo versus *Halo 2*.

✓ Strongly opinionated about Daytime Emmys.

✓ Has never filed a tax return.

✓ You never spend any time at his place. I mean,
  his mom's place.

Should you break up with him? If you want to, you'll have to do
it yourself, because he'll never get around to it.

HOW TO TELL IF YOUR BOYFRIEND IS
A TIME TRAVELER FROM THE PAST

✓ Is dumbfounded by your globe.

✓ Gets aroused when he catches a glimpse of your ankles.

✓ Seems disappointed that you're less than knowledgeable about Cold War relations.

✓ Obsessed with the History Channel.

Should you break up with him? A random fissure in the fabric of time brought you two together. Destiny? Well, that's a romantic idea. But there are a few practical considerations to work out before you get in too deep. First, on the off chance that you're soulmates, one of you is going to have to roll the dice and leave your current life behind. Possible consequences: famine, war, marrying your own dad. You've seen *Back to the Future*. That stuff's all interconnected. But if you're willing to risk it all, do yourself a favor and insist that he remain in this era. Previous centuries will be about as welcoming to you as the Taliban.

HOW TO TELL IF YOUR BOYFRIEND IS
A MISANTHROPE

✓ You had to make the first move.

✓ Does not agree that Disneyland is the happiest place on earth.

✓ Gets most of his grocery shopping done between 2 and 4 a.m.

✓ Won't snuggle.

✓ Had a vasectomy at nineteen.

✓ You met when you were lost in the woods and happened to stumble upon his shack.

Should you break up with him? Don't you feel special? He hates the entire human race. Except you! That's a 1 in 6,493,284,681 chance. You must be his soulmate. Keep him.

HOW TO TELL IF YOUR BOYFRIEND IS
A MISOGYNIST

✓ Owns all the *Girls Gone Wild* DVDs.

✓ Wants to know why you only hang out with whores.

✓ Prefers Asian chicks because they know how to treat a man.

✓ Believes men are from Mars, women are from Hades.

✓ He had you at "Yo, bitch."

Should you break up with him? Every girl loves a challenge. Maybe you're the one who can change his mind about an entire gender. Come on. He'd only trust another guy's opinion about something that serious. Anyway, why don't you just relax and let the man be who he is? Are you on your period or something?

See also: Pimp, p. 18; Serial Killer, p. 26

HOW TO TELL IF YOUR BOYFRIEND IS
ACTUALLY A WOMAN

✓ You've never seen his "penis" in broad daylight.

✓ *C'est la vie* attitude about birth control.

✓ Claims to be allergic to blow jobs.

✓ Your periods are in sync.

Should you break up with her? Technically, she is a liar. But she probably just wanted to get you to fall for her *before* she came out to you. That's understandable, right? She knew you were straight. So she must really like you! And lesbianism is really in right now. At the very least, you'll have some hot stories to tell your next boyfriend. What do you have to lose? You're already bi.

HOW TO TELL IF YOUR BOYFRIEND IS
IN THE WITNESS PROTECTION PROGRAM

✓ Doesn't always respond to his "name."

✓ Personal history prior to 1999 seems improvised.

✓ Foreplay feels more like a pat down.

✓ Complains that he cannot find a decent marinara anywhere in Nebraska.

Should you break up with him? If you feel like you don't know who he really is, you're absolutely right. Not the best way to start out a new romance, as trust is the cornerstone of any relationship. And his former associates certainly would have something to say about his trustworthiness, wouldn't they?

Still, you would be able to spend every holiday with your family, since he's not allowed to contact his. It's your call.

See also: Suffering from Amnesia, p. 17

HOW TO TELL IF YOUR BOYFRIEND IS
PASSIVE-AGGRESSIVE

✓ Got lost on the way to pick up your anniversary gift.

✓ Your grocery list is yet another attempt to "control" him.

✓ Telling him to have a nice day is yet another attempt to control him.

✓ In his free time, he enjoys sulking and pouting.

Should you break up with him? He's so-o-o-o hungry, but too tired to cook. Sigh. Really, he'll just throw together a sandwich and he'll be *fine*, just fine. But damn, he's hungry. And he has been feeling a little run down, he should really take care of himself, especially if you want to go out this weekend . . . no, no, no you don't have to cook for him! You had a long day too, that's not why he . . . well, do you really want to? Wow, that would be *awesome*! You make the best chicken ever. He loves you. Yeah, break up.

HOW TO TELL IF YOUR BOYFRIEND IS
A CULT LEADER

✓ He's got issues with authority figures.

✓ You feel strangely submissive around him.

✓ His friends are great, but it's hard to get a little one-on-one time.

✓ It seems like he's only after one thing: your free will.

Should you break up with him? He's a total alpha male, and that can be a real turn-on, no question about it. But you really must break up before your next group date gets too intense. What if all the other couples are swallowing cyanide? Can you stand up to that kind of pressure? If you can, you're not really his type. Dump him.

See also: Narcissist, p. 79; Scientologist, p. 31

HOW TO TELL IF YOUR BOYFRIEND IS
SUFFERING FROM AN ANXIETY DISORDER

✓ Startles when you blink.

✓ Has a prescription for Xanax but is scared to actually take any.

✓ Insists on wearing two condoms, if it's all right with you.

✓ Wears SPF 45 every day—and every night.

✓ Checks for lumps while he's fondling your breasts.

Should you break up with him? He's eager to please, isn't he? Always fretting about whether you like the restaurant he's chosen or whether your orgasm was authentic or not. Sweet. At first, anyway. But after a while his constant whining will grate on you like Parmesan. Deep down you know it, too. So go ahead and just break up already. He's always known it would never last.

HOW TO TELL IF YOUR BOYFRIEND IS
A ZOMBIE

✓ His look is kind of grunge.

✓ Dry, flaky skin; unruly hair.

✓ Putrefaction is causing major B.O.

✓ Hard to impress.

✓ Chunks of your flesh are rapidly disappearing.

Should you break up with him? You should. This guy is only after your body. His lust for flesh is all-consuming. But don't worry, he's not the brightest bulb, so a breakup merely involves running like hell. Fortunately, he's easily distracted, so disappear into the nearest crowd. Chances are he'll find someone there who will satisfy him just as well.

See also: Bipolar, p. 82

HOW TO TELL IF YOUR BOYFRIEND IS
A POLYGAMIST

✓ He has twenty-eight kids.

✓ No problem with commitment.

✓ Surprisingly willing to wait for sex.

✓ You're fifteen.

Should you break up with him? Yes. He considers himself a man of God, so put it to him this way: God never intended for twelve women to share a single penis. Especially such a small one.

HOW TO TELL IF YOUR BOYFRIEND IS
AN EX-CONVICT

✓ Uncomfortable in wide open spaces.

✓ Tattoos your name on his knuckles with a Bic pen and a lighter.

✓ Offers to trade cigarettes for sex.

Should you break up with him? It all depends. A hardened con who's been inside for ten or more years will generally be too set in his ways to be good boyfriend material. But a one-time offender who's served anywhere from three to six, with time off for good behavior, could be quite a catch. He will be grateful for any small attention you bestow. He's used to staying close to home, performing menial tasks, and generally doing as he's told. Keep him.

HOW TO TELL IF YOUR BOYFRIEND IS
TOO OLD FOR YOU

✓ Can't be on top until he gets his hip replacement.

✓ Makes dinner reservations for 4:30.

✓ Urinates fifty times a day.

✓ His "ATV" looks suspiciously like a HoverRound.

✓ You feel compelled to check on him during a
   heat wave.

Should you break up with him? So your daddy didn't love you.
But that's not your fault! Well, probably not, anyway. Don't punish
yourself by exclusively doing geezers. Get some therapy and find yourself a man with a prostate and some muscle tone. You deserve it.

HOW TO TELL IF YOUR BOYFRIEND IS
A RAGEAHOLIC

✓ Tries to pass off "dumbass" as a pet name.

✓ Your friends are alarmed at the increase in freak accidents you're experiencing.

✓ It's his goddamn fucking house, and he'll leave the goddamn fucking toilet seat up if he wants to.

✓ He's pissed about those court-ordered anger management classes.

Should you break up with him? You should definitely break up. Maybe he'll change someday, maybe he won't, but you can't afford to wait it out. Work on your self-esteem and stop banging your head against this particular wall. Or, you know, his fist.

See also: Possessed by Demons, p. 57; Trying to Kill You, p. 103

HOW TO TELL IF YOUR BOYFRIEND IS
A JUNKIE

✓ Keeps an adrenaline shot at your place.

✓ Brags about the time he was declared legally dead.

✓ You met him in a pawn shop.

✓ Maintains a boyish figure, despite rarely working out.

✓ Thinks the propaganda about sharing needles is a ploy by the needle marketing people.

Should you break up with him? This guy is going to have a problem with boundaries—as in the boundaries between him and every material possession you own. At some point, he will need to sell them all to satisfy his insatiable craving for smack. You can either break up now or after he sells your stuff. Either way, change your locks.

See also: On Crystal Meth, p. 75

HOW TO TELL IF YOUR BOYFRIEND IS
AN ILLEGAL ALIEN

✓ Lives in a two-bedroom with seventeen roommates.

✓ Keeps "misplacing" his visa.

✓ Is pumped about his new job at the slaughterhouse.

✓ Doesn't believe in long engagements.

Should you break up with him? Don't rush into anything with some mad, impetuous illegal alien. Of course, it's in his best interest to marry you right away. But what's in it for you? Great sex? Lasting love and commitment? Children? Jewelry? Whatever it is, make sure you get it before you get married. Because once the government is satisfied that your marriage is legit, his citizenship is nonrefundable. And your leverage is gone.

HOW TO TELL IF YOUR BOYFRIEND IS
POSSESSED BY DEMONS

✓ Sometimes you feel like you don't know him at *all*.

✓ He can be quite the potty mouth.

✓ Terrible acid reflux.

✓ Red-eye episodes not limited to photographs.

✓ You have to be on top so he doesn't levitate.

Should you break up with him? You don't have to break up—you just have to find a good exorcist to tackle this problem. But check references thoroughly, as your boyfriend could die if his exorcist sucks. And under no circumstances should you attempt to perform the exorcism yourself—expelling demons is not like fixing a leaky faucet.

See also: Actually Twins, p. 19; Suffering from Multiple Personality Disorder, p. 62

HOW TO TELL IF YOUR BOYFRIEND IS
A WORKAHOLIC

✓ You've doubled with his office cleaning lady and her husband.

✓ He's sent or received a fax during intercourse.

✓ Your naked ass has touched a cubicle wall.

Should you break up with him? You can be the patient, understanding partner, making do with the time he has available, spending nights and weekends alone, and foregoing vacations altogether. But men who slave away their twenties and thirties often wake up later in life and realize they've missed out on a lot of fun. So when they finally arrive at the top, with a nice salary and more personal freedom, they hook up with a twenty-three-year-old and make up for lost time. Where does that leave you? Lonely, bitter, used up. And cracking open the chardonnay just a little bit earlier each day.

Break up and find yourself a more balanced man while you're young and hopeful. And your drinking is still is purely recreational.

See also: Renegade Cop, p. 58; Cult Leader, p. 44; Stalker, p. 73; Robot, p. 30

HOW TO TELL IF YOUR BOYFRIEND IS
A PEDOPHILE

✓ He's a foster parent/scoutmaster/teacher/
priest/coach.

✓ Gets inappropriate with Tickle Me Elmo.

✓ Sweats profusely at your cousin's bris.

✓ Has to alert the state when he moves.

✓ Fruit Roll-Ups on the nightstand.

Should you break up with him? Not if you prefer a lover who considers your naked body a grotesque distortion of the ideal. But if you want that kind of affirmation, just go shopping for jeans. That way you're the only one who gets hurt.

The hard truth is that the man is suffering through sex with you while crushing on a Webelo. You're merely a cover that will allow him to pursue his freakish desires without arousing suspicion. Break up, and take a long shower.

See also: Polygamist, p. 49

HOW TO TELL IF YOUR BOYFRIEND IS
A BUMPKIN

✓ Couch on the porch.

✓ His first wife is also his first cousin.

✓ Owns his own hog. And it's not a bike.

✓ Asks the waiter if the cacciatore can be prepared with squirrel.

✓ Wears that trucker hat without a trace of irony.

Should you break up with him? The bumpkin has a homespun charm and a refreshingly simple outlook on life, but a future together is risky at best. Unfortunately, in this case, you have to consider the delicate issue of inbreeding. A close family is good, but there's such thing as *too* close. Remember, it's up to you to be the lifeguard of your own gene pool. Think of your potential descendants, and look for another boyfriend.

See also: Gun Nut, p. 100

HOW TO TELL IF YOUR BOYFRIEND IS
SUFFERING FROM MULTIPLE PERSONALITY DISORDER

✓ Has no idea why he bought that mandolin.

✓ Is as surprised as you are to find that human head in his freezer.

✓ His dog's weight has tripled in recent months.

✓ Runs like a girl.

Should you break up with him? Which one? You can't really have a successful relationship with a fraction of a personality, unless you're Tipper Gore. Just stop showing up for dates. He'll assume his seventeenth-century New England minister personality drowned you. He always did think you were a witch.

See also: Actually Twins, p. 19; Bipolar, p. 82; Possessed by Demons, p. 57

HOW TO TELL IF YOUR BOYFRIEND IS
A PLAYER

✓ During arguments, accuses you of being a player-hater.

✓ Can't believe how much your mom looks like you from behind.

✓ Lipstick on his penis is not your shade.

✓ You are the most paranoid person he's ever met.

Should you break up with him? Don't hate the player, hate yourself. Look what you've become! Suspicious, irritable. Soon you'll have carpal tunnel from checking the "recent calls" log on his phone, and you'll be lying awake nights trying to figure out which of your friends he's screwing. Break up. And make some new friends of your own. Male friends.

See also: Pimp, p. 18

HOW TO TELL IF YOUR BOYFRIEND IS
A FUGITIVE
FROM JUSTICE

✓ Walks quickly in the opposite direction when hailed on the street.

✓ Refuses to participate in karaoke.

✓ Cash only, no exceptions.

✓ Constantly asking you if he looks nondescript enough.

Should you break up with him? It depends. If you're spontaneous and you like to travel, you may well enjoy the life the Fugitive from Justice can offer you. Be warned that it won't be four-star accommodations, though, as life without two forms of valid ID can be a real financial challenge.

HOW TO TELL IF YOUR BOYFRIEND IS
JEALOUS

✓ Doesn't know why you have to *look* at the waiter when you order.

✓ You can't tell if he's kidding about the burka.

✓ Uses a new ceiling fan as an excuse to install a ho-cam over your bed.

✓ Hates the game, but also holds the player personally responsible.

Should you break up with him? Why should his relentless interrogation bother you? That is, if you're not doing anything wrong. Guilty conscience? You should be thanking your boyfriend for being so attentive. Isn't that what every woman wants? And by the way, you would look much prettier without all that crap on your face.

See also: Stalker, p. 73; Control Freak, p. 94; Rageaholic, p. 52; Pimp, p. 18; Misogynist, p. 39

HOW TO TELL IF YOUR BOYFRIEND IS
A HIT MAN

✓ You're afraid to leave him alone with your old,
   crippled dog.

✓ Buys lime in bulk at the garden center.

✓ Your boss has a broken nose and treats you with
   newfound respect.

Should you break up with him? He's not afraid to call the shots.
And he never bores you with talk about his latest PowerPoint presentation, which is certainly refreshing. Overall, he's got a sexy, dangerous
edge. So go ahead and have some fun! If nothing else, he's discreet.
But there's really no future in his line of work—no company credit card,
no retirement benefits. Not even a tax refund. So don't take things too
seriously. And end it sooner rather than later. If he decides to eliminate
you, things could really get messy.

See also: Serial Killer, p. 26; Trying to Kill You, p. 103

HOW TO TELL IF YOUR BOYFRIEND IS
MARRIED WITH CHILDREN

✓ Crumbs in the backseat.

✓ Takes you to T.G.I. Friday's for your birthday.

✓ Wears novelty boxer shorts.

✓ Automatically takes out your trash after you have sex because he assumes it's Tuesday.

✓ Care Bears bandage on his shaving cut.

Should you break up with him? He's obviously not afraid of commitment, though it's not like he values it, either. But it's different with you, honestly. You're not like his wife, bugging him to save for retirement, take the kids to practice, blah, blah, blah. You know the real him. The sexy, fun, adventurous him. Marry him! Wait, you can't. Well, he'll leave her. He just has to wait for the right time. Be patient.

See also: Total Bastard, p. 23; Suffering from Multiple Personality Disorder, p. 62; Polygamist, p. 49

HOW TO TELL IF YOUR BOYFRIEND IS
A GHOST

✓ Always turning up unexpectedly.

✓ Appears as a hazy white spot in photos.

✓ Has a message from your grandpa.

✓ A pocket of cold air envelopes him at all times.

Should you break up with him? Time and space have made this decision for you. It's not meant to be. Your boyfriend has simply not accepted the idea that he's dead. Loudly inform him of that fact and instruct him to go toward the light. Then find yourself a man with a little more substance.

HOW TO TELL IF YOUR BOYFRIEND IS
AN ALCOHOLIC

✓ Drank your nail polish remover during a snowstorm.

✓ Turned his glove compartment into a minibar.

✓ He's bidding on new livers.

✓ Banned for life from your office holiday party.

✓ You have a special pail you keep by the bed when he sleeps over.

Should you break up with him? Have the serenity to accept what you cannot change—your boyfriend is a drunk. Right now, he's fun, he's wild, he's the life of the party. But in a few years he'll be a bloated, angry, unemployed loser, stealing small bills from your purse to buy a pint and picking fights at family get-togethers. Break up.

HOW TO TELL IF YOUR BOYFRIEND IS
A STALKER

✓ That waiter you flirt with at the coffee shop has gone missing.

✓ Thinks it's sweet when you file your first restraining order.

✓ Wants another telephoto lens for his birthday.

✓ Punches out your dad for calling you his best girl.

Should you break up with him? It would be ideal to break up, because he probably won't ever be able to give you the space you need. But, come on, he'll never let you leave him! So why not make the most of the situation? He's totally into you.

HOW TO TELL IF YOUR BOYFRIEND IS
A PSYCHIC

✓ It's like he can read your mind.

✓ Never asks about your sexual fantasies, but is strangely in tune with them.

✓ Gets pissed at you for no apparent reason.

✓ Rarely bothers to vote.

Should you break up with him? Being with this guy can have its advantages. You know who your true friends are, what routes to avoid during rush hour, and when those shoes are going to go on sale. But he can be a bit of a know-it-all. And with all the dead people he's seeing, it can seem like there's no time for you. It's a tough call, but just relax and follow his lead. He probably already knows how this is going to end.

See also: Extraterrestrial, p. 20; Angel, p. 84

HOW TO TELL IF YOUR BOYFRIEND IS
ON CRYSTAL METH

✓ You love him more with your headphones on.

✓ His slight frame collapses under the weight of a heavy sweater.

✓ You initially thought he was bilingual, but his second language turned out to be gibberish.

✓ Sleeps on the first and fifteenth of every month.

✓ You save a ton of money on food, because he only eats Skittles.

Should you break up with him? It seems like you two can talk for hours on end. No wait, that's just him. You're really more of a listener, aren't you? Well, at least one of you will know what the hell he was talking about.

HOW TO TELL IF YOUR BOYFRIEND IS
A CROSS-DRESSER

✓ Wishes he had a smaller penis so he could get a smoother line under knits.

✓ You find an unfamiliar lipstick in the bathroom and hope that he's cheating on you.

✓ Asks you to spot him for VPL.

✓ Knows what silk charmeuse is.

✓ You're not sure if he's fondling your breast or your sweater.

Should you break up with him? Granted, it's a little freaky. But think about it. If he wears the same size as you and has even semi-decent taste, this could be a win-win. You both instantly double your wardrobe. And imagine not having to hide your clothing purchases in the trunk of your car until you can safely sneak them into your closet, snip off the tags, and pretend they're not new. Because the Cross-Dresser will understand why you had to buy yet another pair of black pants. Liberating, right? And frankly, a guy who can appreciate your flair for accessorizing is not that easy to come by. Give him/her a chance.

HOW TO TELL IF YOUR BOYFRIEND IS
A NYMPHOMANIAC

✓ On weekends, you rarely bother dressing below the waist.

✓ Chafing is becoming a major issue in your life.

✓ Your public displays of affection qualify as misdemeanors.

✓ You initiate threesomes so you can get some rest.

✓ The spare room is used for condom storage.

Should you break up with him? Well, there's nothing wrong with a hot romance. But with the nympho, after a while, you may start to feel like a receptacle. It's a bit impersonal, isn't it? All he really needs is a girl who can match his stamina. Hang in there for as long as you want, but break up before you fall in love. At heart, the nympho is really not a one-woman man. But you will have some wild memories. And maybe a new fuck buddy?

HOW TO TELL IF YOUR BOYFRIEND IS
A NARCISSIST

✓ During sex with you, he fantasizes that he's masturbating.

✓ Buys you mirrored sunglasses.

✓ Doesn't understand what the big deal is about Johnny Depp.

✓ Frequently wonders if you realize who you're dealing with.

✓ Calls out his own name during orgasm.

Should you break up with him? If this relationship were a porn film, you would be the fluffer—you're responsible for constantly stroking his ego, and your needs are really immaterial as long as you get the job done. Not very rewarding work. But unlike the fluffer, you will be screwed in the end. Break up. Just tell him you're not good enough for him. He won't argue with that.

HOW TO TELL IF YOUR BOYFRIEND IS
ADDICTED TO PORN

✓ The remote is sticky again.

✓ So is the keyboard.

✓ And the phone.

Should you break up with him? Sure, porn can be part of a healthy relationship. But when your boyfriend complains that sex with you cuts into his wanking time, you have a problem. He prefers fantasy to reality. So unless you're willing to settle for fantasy orgasms, break up. He'll know exactly what to do with all that extra time on his hands.

HOW TO TELL IF YOUR BOYFRIEND IS
BIPOLAR

✓ Everything's black or white with him.

✓ Built an authentic Japanese pagoda in the yard in an hour and a half. Then burned it to the ground.

✓ Sleeps every other week.

✓ Owns a Hummer *and* a Prius.

✓ Tears of pain mix freely with tears of joy.

Should you break up with him? He's such a drama queen, and that can be exhausting. Try to get him on some medication and see if it helps. If you still don't feel it's working out, break up. But do it during his down cycle, when he won't have the strength to argue with you.

See also: Suffering from Multiple Personality Disorder, p. 62; Actually Twins, p. 19

HOW TO TELL IF YOUR BOYFRIEND IS
A MAMA'S BOY

✓ Asks you to wear a nursing bra.

✓ Dad and stepdad both died under mysterious circumstances.

✓ Picks fights hoping you'll spank him.

✓ Has a "Mom" tattoo, but it's on his ass.

✓ His Pampers make a squishing sound when he walks.

Should you break up with him? A man who is good to his mother is nice. A man who is obsessed with his mother is better off single. You'll never measure up to Mommy. Break up. And remember not to do that to your son, if you ever have one.

HOW TO TELL IF YOUR BOYFRIEND IS
AN ANGEL

✓ A sense of calm and joy overcomes you in his presence.

✓ "Mean people suck" bumper sticker.

✓ You met on Christmas Eve when you were on the edge of the bridge contemplating suicide.

✓ Doesn't go in for sarcasm or heavy petting.

✓ Radiant complexion.

Should you break up with him? You're not really calling the shots in this relationship, so relax. Apparently, you're part of a much larger plan, and you're about to mess it up by doing something stupid. It could be that an evil national corporation will take over your candy shop and corrupt the old-fashioned values of your hometown. Or you could invoke nuclear war and annihilate the human race. Whatever. Your boyfriend is intervening to prevent imminent disaster. It seems that fate has to take the form of a cute guy for you to pay attention. So maybe your lesson is to cultivate a little more depth? You'll have to stay with him to figure that out.

HOW TO TELL IF YOUR BOYFRIEND IS
A GOVERNMENT-TRAINED ASSASSIN

✓ No discernible sense of humor.

✓ Juliennes vegetables with great precision.

✓ His office never has any happy hours.

✓ You haven't seen squirrels in the yard in quite some time.

✓ His drop-in visitors are often seriously wounded.

Should you break up with him? It depends on the level of intimacy you're looking for. The Government-Trained Assassin is not really the kind of a guy who will pour out his heart and soul to you (unless you've been issued the appropriate security clearance by the government). Are you ready for that kind of a background check? Plus, he's kind of intense. Don't ever sneak up behind him, playfully cover his eyes, and ask him to guess who it is. That would be the quickest way to end things, but definitely not the smartest.

HOW TO TELL IF YOUR BOYFRIEND IS
DYSLEXIC

✓ Sucks at Scrabble.

✓ Asks you to sketch what you need from the grocery store.

✓ Subtitles "hurt his eyes."

✓ Always burns the microwave popcorn.

✓ Thinks you could be his life-meat.

Should you break up with him? How much reading is actually involved in a relationship? As long as you balance the checkbook and translate recipes and directions into rebus for him, you have a real chance at making this work. Stay.

See also: Illegal Alien, p. 55; Bumpkin, p. 60

HOW TO TELL IF YOUR BOYFRIEND IS
A RENEGADE COP

✓ Even if he's just making toast, he's going to do it his way.

✓ Smokes four packs a day.

✓ Is self-conscious about going shirtless because his torso is riddled with bullet scars.

✓ Sports a late-eighties *Lethal Weapon* mullet.

Should you break up with him? It takes a strong woman to handle the Renegade Cop's devotion to the job. You'd better have a full schedule, because he won't be home for dinner. Instead, he'll be out on the streets keeping decent citizens safe from skels, scumbags, and all manner of perps. And if he has to bend a few rules to put those assholes away, so be it. His demeanor is gruff, his tactics unorthodox, but he's got a heart of gold. So if you want him, don't play hard to get. The risky undercover work, top-speed car chases, and drug lords with axes to grind give him an average lifespan of about thirty-eight years.

HOW TO TELL IF YOUR BOYFRIEND IS
CLINICALLY DEPRESSED

✓ Did he sigh? He didn't realize.

✓ Buys you a vibrator so you won't bug him to have sex anymore.

✓ Wears the wristbands because it looks cool, not to cover the scar tissue.

✓ You are lulled to sleep each night by the sound of his gentle weeping.

Should you break up with him? He's a very sensitive soul. But a little of that goes a long way, as you're probably finding out. You have a man capable of great feeling. Though perhaps part of what he is feeling is a slight chemical imbalance. If you can rein that in, you just may have a sweet, sensitive boyfriend. Or you may have a catatonic, impotent couch potato. Sometimes you need to adjust the dosage on those medications. Anyway, you may as well give it a shot. You've put up with him so far.

HOW TO TELL IF YOUR BOYFRIEND IS
SUFFERING
FROM AN STD

✓ Tries to convince you it's just genital acne.

✓ Screams when he urinates.

✓ Has to wait for the ointment to dry before he can put on his shorts.

✓ Catching up a lot lately with old lovers, and urges you to do the same.

✓ Looks nervous when you comment on his infectious laugh.

Should you break up with him? Well, it depends. Did you consider your relationship to be exclusive? Because it looks like *he* didn't. Needless to say, if you did, break up. If you weren't at that point yet, find out his prognosis before you make any hasty decisions. Anyone can make a mistake, right? So, if he's curable and still has a respectable sperm count, perhaps it is time to set up some boundaries in this relationship. Spell out what you need and give him a second chance. But first, get yourself a Pap smear.

HOW TO TELL IF YOUR BOYFRIEND IS
A NARCOLEPTIC

✓ Frequently asks you to repeat yourself.

✓ Sometimes you feel like he's just not there for you.

✓ Face often soiled.

Should you break up with him? This relationship can work—it's just a matter of adjusting your expectations. Go to shorter movies. Schedule frequent naps. Be concise with conversation. And above all, do the driving yourself.

See also: Suffering from ADHD, p. 25

HOW TO TELL IF YOUR BOYFRIEND IS
A CONTROL FREAK

✓ Wants to have a dress rehearsal before you meet his parents.

✓ Pencils you in for a little spontaneity next Tuesday.

✓ Lays out your clothes for you each night.

✓ Storyboards new sex acts, just so you're on the same page.

Should you break up with him? If anyone knows whether you two should break up, it's your boyfriend. He's steered this thing so far, hasn't he?

See also: Cult Leader, p. 44

HOW TO TELL IF YOUR BOYFRIEND IS
P-WHIPPED

✓ Knows that the Tampax in the green wrapper is the Super.

✓ Holds your purse, even when your hands are free.

✓ Fetches Diet Cokes on command.

✓ His scrotum looks suspiciously empty.

Should you break up with him? If you love something, set it free. If it's yours, it will return to you. If it just stares blankly at you and awaits further instruction, then you've crushed its spirit. And if recovery is at all possible, it will take a kinder, gentler partner than you to facilitate it. So break up and find someone else. Only this time, let him retain a little dignity.

HOW TO TELL IF YOUR BOYFRIEND IS
ON STEROIDS

✓ You envy his cleavage.

✓ He's constantly asking if that guy's bigger than him.

✓ Beat Mickey Mantle's home-run record.

✓ Cannot touch his own ass.

✓ His testicles have shriveled like raisins.

Should you break up with him? He just wants to be huge. Is that so wrong? Well, it's sort of the inverse of the thin-obsessed female. And you know how annoying *she* is. Except she's too weak and hungry to kick your ass, and your boyfriend isn't. Break up by phone in case the 'roid rage kicks in.

See also: Rageaholic, p. 52

HOW TO TELL IF YOUR BOYFRIEND IS
A HOMOPHOBE

✓ Has a barber.

✓ Limits physical contact with other males to punching and shoving.

✓ Will not hold your purse under any circumstances.

✓ Washes his hair with a bar of soap, because shampoo is too femme.

✓ Two thumbs down on *Brokeback Mountain*.

Should you break up with him? The homophobe is intent on proving his manhood. That can be hot, for a while. But actually, he's terrified of his own sexuality. And that's kind of gay, isn't it?

See also: Bumpkin, p. 60; Misanthrope, p. 38

HOW TO TELL IF YOUR BOYFRIEND IS
A COMPULSIVE GAMBLER

✓ He's had six knee replacements.

✓ Bet you he could make you go out with him!

✓ Got two dollars off your nephew playing Candyland.

✓ Keeps losing his ATM card; could you spot him a hundred?

✓ You have attended a cockfight.

Should you break up with him? What you need for this relationship to work is a little foresight. Sometimes you have to spend a little money to make a little money. This guy is laying the groundwork for a secure future for you two. When his horse comes in, as it inevitably will, he'll never have to gamble again. Oh sure, that's what every guy hanging out at the OTB says. But they don't have his handicapping system.

HOW TO TELL IF YOUR BOYFRIEND IS
A GUN NUT

✓ You can have the last piece of chicken when you pry it from his cold, dead fingers.

✓ Considers any education beyond eighth grade extraneous.

✓ Tenderly asks to store some ammo at your place.

✓ Frequently remarks that guns don't kill people, *people* kill people.

Should you break up with him? This guy is very passionate, and it's easy to get swept up in that. Flowers, candy, monogrammed holsters. But what happens when you accidentally shrink his Toby Keith "Boot in Your Ass" tour T-shirt and he starts screaming about his right to protect his laundry? Do you feel comfortable standing up to a man with more weapons than books? Think about it. Wait for a time when he's unarmed, and break up. Then get yourself a Kevlar vest. Just until he meets someone new.

See also: Bumpkin, p. 60

HOW TO TELL IF YOUR BOYFRIEND IS
A VAMPIRE

✓ Can be kind of a leech.

✓ Hints that your crucifix makes you look fat.

✓ Doesn't show up in photos.

✓ Turned off by turtlenecks.

Should you break up with him? What is it about those strangely hypnotic eyes? You feel powerless to resist. In no time at all, this man will declare his undying love for you. But the vampire's "love" can quickly become overwhelming. Soon it will begin to feel like he's sucking the life right out of you. You have to leave him. And unfortunately, you're looking at a messy breakup. You can't just evade the guy's phone calls and hope he gets the hint. In this case, a specific plan of attack is absolutely necessary. So follow these instructions exactly.

First, wear something you hate, because you're going to totally ruin it. Next, go to the hardware store and ask for a large wooden stake. Make sure you can wield it easily. Okay, once you've found the right stake, take it home and drive it straight through your boyfriend's heart. Then sever his head completely. Finally, burn his body and immediately scatter or bury the ashes at a crossroads.

Now go treat yourself to a long, hot bath. You've earned it, girl!

HOW TO TELL IF YOUR BOYFRIEND IS
TRYING TO KILL YOU

✓ Can't wait to show you how to play the choking game.

✓ Sleeps most comfortably with his pillow over your face.

✓ Interested to learn you're not a strong swimmer.

✓ Likes to clean his gun near your head.

Should you break up with him? Only you and he really know if you deserve to be killed. Are you rich? Unfaithful? A castrating bitch? Pregnant? Or all of the above? Regardless, it's time for a heart-to-heart. What you really have is a communication problem. Listen to what he needs from the relationship and impress upon him your strong will to live. Maybe you can meet each other halfway. Actually, insist that he meet you *all* the way. And if he agrees, give him one more chance. After that, if he "didn't know it was loaded," go on and prosecute to the fullest extent of the law.

HOW TO TELL IF YOUR BOYFRIEND IS
AGORAPHOBIC

✓ You met him on your FedEx delivery route.

✓ You never do it at your place.

✓ He buys, you fly, no exceptions.

✓ You can't tell what kind of car he drives because it's obscured by cobwebs.

Should you break up with him? At first it can be cozy, staying in, just the two of you, in your little love cocoon. But sooner or later you'll feel like some sushi, and your boyfriend will be afraid to go get some. You're a sensitive person, but inevitably you'll grow to resent him and his sorry homemade maki rolls. It's not your fault. You're only human. And you're too good-looking to be sequestered, anyway.

See also: Misanthrope, p. 38; Fugitive from Justice, p. 65

HOW TO TELL IF YOUR BOYFRIEND IS
AN INSUFFERABLE BORE

✓ Thinks you're a super lady.

✓ Wants to know who moved his cheese.

✓ John Tesh concert tee.

✓ Makes his dog wear a bandanna.

✓ Has a heart of hearts.

Should you break up with him? Break up, unless you suffer from severe and persistent insomnia—in which case this man is a godsend.

See also: Trekkie, p. 33; Scientologist, p. 31

HOW TO TELL IF YOUR BOYFRIEND IS
A CRACKHEAD

✓ Significant lack of interest in non-crack-related activities.

✓ Loose standards of personal hygiene.

✓ Has a group of his friends squatting in your shed.

✓ Will beat any price for a blow job.

Should you break up with him? The rock is a demanding mistress. She calls at all hours. Your boyfriend is ready and willing to answer—and you will need to be equally committed to winning him away from her, if that's what you want. Tracking him down to seedy apartments, paying off his debts, shooing away his toothless cronies. You're in for quite a fight! Are you sure it's worth the trouble? Because even if you do win, the prize is a crackhead. Can't you do any better than that?

HOW TO TELL IF YOUR BOYFRIEND IS
A PATHOLOGICAL LIAR

✓ Fakes orgasms.

✓ Excess weight is due to the fact that he's "half bulimic."

✓ Has proof there are WMDs in Iraq.

✓ Part Cherokee.

✓ Working undercover at Kinko's to bust a counterfeiting ring.

Should you break up with him? Is trust important? Interesting question. Has that issue ever been explored in a romantic context? Let's go out on a limb and hypothesize that, indeed, trust can be critical in an intimate relationship. In fact, some would consider it the very basis of a solid union. So where does that leave you? Living in a house built on sand. With a big fat liar. So break up and do not waver under any circumstances, even if he only has three months to live. Especially if he only has three months to live.

See also: Actually a Woman, p. 41; Actually Twins, p. 19

INDEX BY TRAIT

Not sure of your boyfriend's personality type? Make a quick diagnosis by looking up his symptoms here.

absent, 22, 26, 49, 54, 58, 63, 67, 68, 70, 81, 86, 89, 99

accent, 20, 36, 55, 57, 62, 102

accident-prone, 57, 71, 92, 99

addict, 54, 71, 81, 107

affectionate, 55, 78, 84

aggressive, 52, 57, 89, 97, 103

ambitious, 11, 58, 103

angry, 39, 52, 89, 97

animals, dislikes, 23, 26, 30, 100

antisocial, 30, 38, 65, 90, 105

anxious, 22, 14, 34, 42, 46, 54, 65, 68, 91, 95, 103

arrogant, 11, 20, 23, 39, 44, 79

authority, trouble with, 11, 20, 23, 38, 39, 44, 79, 89, 100

bad breath, 47, 54, 57, 65, 70, 71, 107

beatific, 17, 44, 84

body hair, 11, 36, 97

boring, 14, 30, 33, 47, 90, 92, 105, 106

catatonic, 30, 47, 54, 82, 90

charismatic, 11, 44, 63, 84, 102

cheap, 23, 35, 36, 39, 65, 107

children, friendly with, 49, 59, 84

clingy, 31, 55, 66, 73, 95

committed, 11, 41, 44, 49, 55, 73

confused, 19, 25, 36, 62, 75, 87

controlling, 20, 23, 43, 44, 94

convulsions, 52, 57

criminal activity, 18, 26, 28, 54, 55, 59, 65, 67, 97, 99, 100, 107

deceptive, 15, 19, 41, 54, 63, 68, 103, 108

digestive issues, 34, 46, 51, 57

disheveled, 35, 47, 54, 65, 107

distracted, 25, 47, 62, 92, 103

domineering, 18, 31, 44, 94

drooling, 47, 81, 92

dusty, 47, 51, 65, 107

Edwardian, 15, 36, 51

egotistical, 44, 79

emaciated, 47, 54, 107

eyes
   crossed, 57, 60
   glazed, 52, 73, 92
   hypnotic, 20, 44, 84, 102
   wandering, 25, 63

feminine, 15, 41, 76, 83
forgetful, 17, 19, 25, 62, 71
friendly, 44, 59, 63, 78, 84
foulmouthed, 18, 52, 57, 66, 97
frail, 51, 70, 75
fun-loving, 59, 63, 78, 91

haircut, bad, 36, 55, 60, 89, 100, 105
hairless, 41, 51, 59
head injury, 17, 52, 70
health issues, 34, 51, 91
hooves, cloven, 11
hygienic, 14
hyperactive, 25, 75, 82

immature, 17, 33, 59, 83
incontinent, 51, 57, 71, 92
indecisive, 19, 25, 62
inferiority complex, 50, 65, 66, 83, 95
intelligence
    high, 20, 74, 108
    lack of, 17, 35, 47, 60, 100

jealous, 39, 52, 66, 73
jumpy, 22, 46, 98, 105

lazy, 35, 92, 105
libido
    high, 19, 33, 78, 98
    lack of, 15, 30, 39, 51, 59, 70, 84, 90, 97
lying. See deceptive

macho, 36, 52, 89, 97, 98
manic, 25, 46, 52, 82, 91
medicated, 14, 34, 46, 54, 71, 82, 90, 91, 107
messy, 28, 47, 57, 81, 92
misshapen, 20, 60, 70
moody, 66, 82, 89, 97, 103
mullet, 60, 89

needy, 27, 35, 41, 43, 54, 73, 83, 102, 105
negative, 22, 38, 39, 42, 46, 50, 52, 65, 86
nerdy, 31, 33, 36, 49, 83
nervous. See jumpy
nocturnal, 20, 54, 65, 76, 102
noisy, 14, 57, 71, 75, 82
nondescript, 65, 103

overweight, 35, 71, 90, 105

passionate, 52, 78, 82, 89, 102
patient, 30, 49, 73, 84, 86
possessive, 11, 31, 44, 52, 66, 73, 94, 102, 105
pouty, 41, 73, 79, 83, 90

repetitive, 17, 19, 25, 51
rude, 23, 25, 38, 39, 57, 71, 97

secretive, 15, 19, 41, 55, 59, 103
self-conscious, 36, 46, 59
self-esteem
    high, 11, 18, 20, 31, 44, 79, 82,

84, 86
low, 50, 54, 82, 90
sensitive, 41, 73, 74, 84, 90
sex
    overly interested in. *See* libido,
        high
    uninterested in. *See* libido, low
silent, 30, 43, 47, 70, 90
skin irritation, 14, 34, 78, 81, 91
slow-witted, 17, 47, 51, 60
smells, 47, 54, 57, 65, 71, 107
soiled, 47, 92, 107
sophistication, lack of, 47, 49, 60,
    89, 100
speech
    rapid, 25, 75
    slurred, 51, 71
    unintelligible, 55, 57
spittle, 52, 60
    See also drooling
spontaneity, dislikes, 65, 94, 105
stealing, 28, 54, 107
sterile, 30, 34, 70, 84
stutter, 52, 97
sulky. *See* pouty
supportive, 27, 41
sweet, 41, 84
supernatural, 20, 70, 74, 84, 102

taste, bad, 18, 31, 60, 100
tearful, 82, 90
teeth
    missing, 60, 92, 107
    pointed, 11, 102

temper, bad. See anger
testicles
    lack of, 41, 68, 83, 95
    shriveled, 51, 97
threatening, 44, 52, 66, 73, 102,
    103
tough guy, 50, 52, 67, 86, 89, 97, 98
transparent, 70
twitchy, 14, 54, 60, 62, 107

underweight. *See* emaciated
unlawful. *See* criminal activity
unphotogenic, 33, 70, 102

violent, 11, 52, 57, 67, 86, 97

warm, 11, 78, 84
wasteful, 14, 17, 23, 35
whimpering, 83, 90, 95

ACKNOWLEDGMENTS

Special thanks to E.C., who was right about most people. Thanks to B.C., for being exceedingly normal.

Thanks to everyone at Quirk who worked on this project. Especially my editor, Melissa, who is passionate about the subtle nuances that make all the difference.

Thanks to Michael Miller for his spot-on illustrations.

Thanks to Dan and everyone at Writers House for the faith.

And special thanks to Meredith Baxter-Birney, Connie Sellecca, Judith Light, Valerie Bertinelli, Joanna Kerns, Delta Burke, Jaclyn Smith, and all the ladies of Lifetime Television. Your pluck is an inspiration.